DISASTERS IN HISTORY

Shackleton
and the Lost Antarctic Expedition

by B. A. Hoena

illustrated by Dave Hoover
and Charles Barnett III

Consultant:

Robert Headland

Archivist and Curator

Scott Polar Research Institute

University of Cambridge, United Kingdom

Capstone
press

Mankato, Minnesota

Graphic Library is published by Capstone Press,
151 Good Counsel Drive, P.O. Box 669, Mankato, Minnesota 56002.
www.capstonepress.com

1 2 3 4 5 6 11 10 09 08 07 06

Library of Congress Cataloging-in-Publication Data
Hoena, B. A.
    Shackleton and the lost Antarctic expedition / by B. A. Hoena; illustrated by Dave Hoover
and Charles Barnett III.
    p. cm.—(Graphic library. Disasters in history)
    Includes bibliographical references.
    ISBN-13: 978-0-7368-5482-5 (hardcover)
    ISBN-10: 0-7368-5482-7 (hardcover)
    1. Shackleton, Ernest Henry, Sir, 1874–1922—Travel—Antarctica—Juvenile literature.
2. Imperial Trans-Antarctic Expedition (1914–1917)—Juvenile literature. 3. Antarctica—
Discovery and exploration—British—Juvenile literature. 4. Endurance (Ship)—Juvenile
literature. I. Hoover, Dave, 1955– ill. II. Barnett, Charles, III, ill. III. Title. IV. Series.
G850 1914 .S53 H63 2006
919.8'904—dc22   2005029848

Summary: In graphic novel format, tells the story of Antarctic explorer Ernest Shackleton and his
    failed attempt to cross the coldest and windiest continent on earth.

Art Direction and Design
Jason Knudson

Storyboard Artist
B. A. Hoena

Production Artist
Alison Thiele

Editor
Erika L. Shores

Editor's note: Direct quotations from primary sources are indicated by a yellow background.

Direct quotations appear on the following pages:
Pages 6, 10, from crewmembers' diaries as quoted in Endurance: Shackleton's Incredible
    Voyage by Alfred Lansing, (Wheaton, Ill.: Tyndale House, 1999).
Pages 12, 15 (bottom), 21, from crewmembers' diaries and letters as quoted in The Endurance:
    Shackleton's Legendary Antarctic Expedition by Caroline Alexander, (New York: Alfred E.
    Knopf, 1998).
Pages 15 (top), 26, 27, from South: A Memoir of the Endurance Voyage by Ernest Shackleton,
    (New York: Carroll & Graf, 1998).

Table of Contents

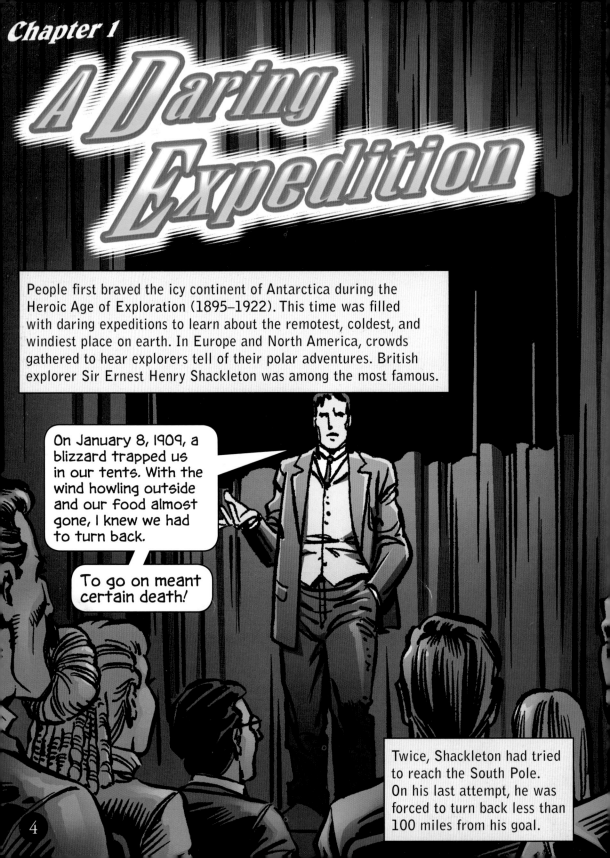

Chapter 1
A Daring Expedition

People first braved the icy continent of Antarctica during the Heroic Age of Exploration (1895–1922). This time was filled with daring expeditions to learn about the remotest, coldest, and windiest place on earth. In Europe and North America, crowds gathered to hear explorers tell of their polar adventures. British explorer Sir Ernest Henry Shackleton was among the most famous.

On January 8, 1909, a blizzard trapped us in our tents. With the wind howling outside and our food almost gone, I knew we had to turn back.

To go on meant certain death!

Twice, Shackleton had tried to reach the South Pole. On his last attempt, he was forced to turn back less than 100 miles from his goal.

The men had little work to do while they waited for warmer weather, but they found ways to keep busy.

Photographer Frank Hurley took pictures of the *Endurance* and her crew . . .

. . . some crewmembers hunted seals for fresh food. . .

. . . and other crewmembers held dogsled races.

During the dark Antarctic winter, the men stayed safe and warm within the ship as blizzards raged outside and temperatures dropped to minus 30 degrees Fahrenheit. Despite the weather, all seemed well.

By the beginning of 1916, the men had used up much of their food supplies. Breakfast consisted of powdered milk and pemmican. For lunch they ate biscuits and a few lumps of sugar. Dinner was their only hot meal. They ate seal and penguin meat.

By the end of March, they had killed all of the dogs to save food.

On April 9, the ice had broken up enough that Shackleton gave the order to launch the boats. But by this time, they had drifted past Paulet Island.

We'll have to head north to Elephant Island, about 50 miles away.

The men rowed between large ice floes and bergs that could easily crush their tiny boats.

Some nights they camped on large ice floes.

Other times they anchored their boats to icebergs. Crewmembers huddled together for warmth.

I can't feel my feet.

Put them under me to keep them from freezing.

The seas between Elephant Island and South Georgia were some of the roughest in the world. Large swells often rose 60 feet or more.

Their small boat provided little protection. The men were constantly wet and cold.

If too much ice builds up on her, she'll sink.

South Georgia was a speck in the vast Southern Ocean. The only way they could find their way was to use the sun to guide them. If Worsley made a mistake navigating, they'd be lost in the endless sea.

I can barely see the sun through that cloud.

More about Ernest Shackleton

Ernest Henry Shackleton was born February 15, 1874, in County Kildare, Ireland. His parents were Abraham and Henrietta Shackleton. Shackleton was the second of 10 children.

In 1901, Shackleton left on his first trip to Antarctica. The National Antarctic Expedition was led by British naval officer Robert Falcon Scott. Scott and Shackleton attempted to find a way to the South Pole. They fell short of their goal by 450 miles.

On April 9, 1904, Shackleton married Emily Dorman. They had two sons, Raymond and Edward, and one daughter, Cecily.

In 1907, Shackleton led an expedition to reach the South Pole. He came within 97 miles of his goal. Shackleton turned back because he and his men were nearly out of supplies. Even though he failed to reach the South Pole, Shackleton was considered a hero for trying. The British king knighted him Sir Ernest Shackleton. Shackleton published a book, *The Heart of the Antarctic*, about his expedition.

In 1911, Robert Falcon Scott and Norwegian explorer Roald Amundsen led separate expeditions to reach the South Pole. Scott was not trained to use dog sleds. He and his men pulled, or "man-hauled," their sleds full of supplies. Amundsen was a skilled dog sled driver. By using dog sleds, he was able to travel twice as fast as Scott. Amundsen reached the South Pole on December 14. Scott and his companions arrived a month later. They died during their return trip from the Pole.

 In 1914, as Shackleton's expedition was about to set sail, fighting broke out in Europe. Great Britain and France went to war with Germany and Austria-Hungary. Shackleton offered the service of his ship and crew to British prime minister Winston Churchill. But Churchill told Shackleton to go on with his expedition.

 In 1921, Shackleton left on what would be his last expedition. While staying on South Georgia, he died of heart failure January 5, 1922, at age 47. He was buried on South Georgia.

Glossary

endurance (en-DUR-uhnss)—the ability to withstand hardships

expedition (ek-spuh-DIH-shuhn)—a journey for purpose of exploration or scientific research

floe (FLOH)—a sheet of floating ice

pemmican (PEM-mi-kuhn)—a mixture of dried meat and fruit

pressure ridge (PREH-shur RIDG)—ice floes that have been upturned from the pressure of pushing against each other

Internet Sites

FactHound offers a safe, fun way to find Internet sites related to this book. All of the sites on FactHound have been researched by our staff.

Here's how:

1. *Visit www.facthound.com*
2. Type in this special code **0736854827** for age-appropriate sites. Or enter a search word related to this book for a more general search.
3. Click on the **Fetch It** button.

FactHound will fetch the best sites for you!

Read More

Calvert, Patricia. *Sir Ernest Shackleton: By Endurance We Conquer.* Great Explorations. New York: Benchmark Books, 2003.

Currie, Stephen. *Antarctica.* Exploration and Discovery. San Diego: Lucent Books, 2004.

Hooper, Meredith. *Antarctic Adventure: Exploring the Frozen South.* New York: DK, 2000.

White, Matt. *Endurance: Shipwreck and Survival on a Sea of Ice.* Mankato, Minn.: Capstone Curriculum Publishing, 2002.

Bibliography

Alexander, Caroline. *The* Endurance*: Shackleton's Legendary Antarctic Expedition.* New York: Alfred E. Knopf, 1998.

Lansing, Alfred. *Endurance: Shackleton's Incredible Voyage.* Wheaton, Ill.: Tyndale House, 1999.

Shackleton, Ernest. *South: A Memoir of the* Endurance *Voyage.* New York: Carroll & Graf, 1998.